Icarus Rising

Misadventures in Ascension

new and selected poems by

Richard Fenton Sederstrom

Published by the Jackpine Writers' Bloc, Inc.

$18.00
ISBN: 978-1-928690-46-7
Published in the United States of America

Published by the Jackpine Writers' Bloc, Inc.
Edited by Sharon Harris
Layout and cover design by Tarah L. Wolff

Cover art, "Portrait of Papa B" (the poet).
Watercolor by Challie Facemire.

Icarus Rising

Misadventures in Ascension

Also by Richard Fenton Sederstrom

Fall Pictures on an Autumn Road

Disordinary Light

Folly: A Book of Last Summers

Eumaeus Tends

Selenity Book Four

Sorgmantel

Acknowledgments

The poet gratefully acknowledges the following magazines as the original publishers of the following poems:

The Blue Guitar Magazine: "Better That" in "Eumaeus Questions the Fossils," "Bison Head in Datil," "The End of Thinking," "The Fourth Deer," "Saint Francis in Biology Class," "Swamp Gas," "Two of Us Talk Mortality." Also the sequence "The Fall of Icarus: Misadventures in Ascension," (Part II in this book).

Dissident Voice: "After Profound Concentration" in "III. In Security Malignant," "At the DMV," "Barrio Alto," "Bottom Dwelling," "Common Gray," "The DTs," "Earth-Bound, Moon-Mad," "Eumaeus Questions the Fossils," "Failing Wings" (poem), "III. In Security Malignant," "Las Moiras" in "VI. Dead Beckoning," "En Musiklärare," "Never Enough Air," "V. The Poor of Atzlan," "A Sunday Afternoon in the Garden of Anthropos," "*Un bel di vedremo.*"

The Talking Stick: "Aspen," "Our Hands," "Some Small Thing, Tan," "Subjective."

Unstrung: "Eumaeus Old and the Magpie," "I Still Dream—After All," "My Life is a key that has finally found its lock," "Schubert's Second Cello." Also an original version of the sequence, "Failing Wings" (Part IV of this book).

Acknowledgments

The nature of one's family will change with time and experience, or maybe only the passive adventure of old age. Eumaeus, Hugh Fenton, Vera Fenton, and I have been approaching a single mind for many years, and I am almost comfortable with the condition. I hope they are.

I have stated before the debt I owe to Alan Johnson, Arthur Colby, and Randel Helms. The current pandemic and our advanced ages prevent our meeting these days, but the nature of our fellowship does not diminish.

I continue to owe my debt of gratitude to Rebecca Dyre and Angie Tibbs for their support of my experiments and eccentricities for all these years. Their encouragement is breath to my spirit.

This book represents the seventh occasion to thank Sharon Harris and Tarah Wolff for their care for me and my work, for their professionalism and artistry. I don't know what relationships are like in the commercial publishing biz, and I don't care to know. With Sharon and Tarah at my back and by my side, I don't need to find out.

And, not finally: my acknowledgment of Challie Facemire, the artist who created the cover "portrait" of the poet, which has graced my study for a couple of decades waiting to be put into public service. The vulture is the bird that grounds the hubris of ascension.

Dedication

As always, this book is for Carol.
It is also for Mrs. Hudson.

To the memory of Nick Salerno

And again, but after only two years, more urgently:

For our children, Carol's and mine, our grandchildren, and our great-grandchildren, I wish you each a peaceful and fulfilling life. More than ever, I fear for each of you and for my wishes.

This dedication goes farther out, to the children of the endangered generations that I will not live to feel for, which I would. My poems exist as the best I can offer you.

The good news is that, even without Anthropos, life will go on in some form, or many forms, dao being . . . well, being what is.

Contents

Contents

III Failing Apogee

IV Failing Wings

Contents

V On Earth

Afterward: Just in Case . . .

But if . . .

A word on the selected poems

I admit to having had thoughts in the past about a volume of Selected Poems. Such a volume should stand as a statement that the poet has made it, has established a reputation worthy of posterity. It is a sign of the poet's stature and maturity. However, I have seen a bit of what "it" is, and I can live otherwise.

I have no reputation worth the altitude, and posterity will so far outlive me that I can't think to recognize the shade of it. And "stature" is a situation fit for good gray poets. I am, I admit, gray, where I have hair at all.

So the notion of a Selected Poems is not appropriate. On the other hand, I have long entertained issues and motifs that I thought might illustrate themselves if I invited some poems into this book that would volunteer to help, poems that have allowed themselves to keep me company for periods from a couple of years to more than a few decades.

Most of them are here in pretty much their original form, not without changes they could agree to, but recognizable from their original publications.

Others, however, found themselves so entwined in the new text that they are no longer recognizable from their original places. We all agree that they prefer their new arrangements, and they are not willing to be newly identified. *Those that are identifiable I have marked with an asterisk in the table of contents.* Because they have agreed to this arrangement and to their new context, they need not be identified further. A poem can live in as many contexts of myth as it cares to.

To consider the mysteries of existence for Sappho's wonders, for one of many examples, might be to consider the nature of Being as art. To the end of that meditation we hope that we have, all of us in our various flights, flutters and stammers, offered something of the human condition: our ways into confusion and the possibility that a door out exists, probably too near to see.

Introduction

from "Codex: A Case for the Lonely Poet"

Engaging in poetry as poet—as reader, as LISTENER, as tolerated if not welcome participant—is engaging with the late simian re-vision of the very beginning, the world before poetry, the world before words. And that return destroys utterly the future of poetry. Only it doesn't; it can't. It does eliminate the possibility of poetry, of any art, even as a profession.

But of course and again, it doesn't. Art, like Walt, is large, a kosmos, and contains multitudes, including professional artists.

*

The artistic life I want to contemplate is the ancient, sacred and disregarded primordium that poets still come from, the old array of human characters who have been driven to look at the world, and beyond the world, in ways that may be accompanied by the ghost of the lyre. Most of us these days seem to have been bred by the fires of MFA programs, like salamanders, but some of us also know that our fires are confined neither to institutions nor myth. We are what we come from:

In Chauvet Cave the little finger of the limned hand is slightly bent. We cannot assume that the hand was chosen on behalf of this trivial misfeature. It is, we assume, a hand communicating—what? It is not our language; we have no language for what we see; we cannot see without language. For us, it is only the bent finger that suggests language—a signature; we cannot help but interpret. It is no more than a flaw, a repeated visual hiccup. If it were speech—poetry—we might hear it, see it, as a stammer, an interruption to the flow of sense that would stop us—and we are stopped—to consider what, in the flow of the poem suddenly sends us beyond language.

*

From *Sorgmantel*: Poetry is the *first breath*, the *ru'ach*, that preceded the actual production of imagined language. Some ancient time ago, a voice at the hearth uttered a meaningful sound divorced from utility, and she and someone else suddenly lost breath and were sent some-no-where entirely new and momently sublime.

But it is in the vocal response, carrying the first sound even further, that the urge to create something new in words alone, for no practical and identifiable purpose—song: poetry—really happened. It still doesn't happen very often; it doesn't last long, but happens, and it recurs.

*

The finger continues to beckon. Some caves are still, to geologists, alive. To the artist, in caves like Chauvet, images still stop us for want of words, including ours. The images and we stand by helplessly stammering and staggeringly unapproachable, and staggeringly alive. Here is a stammer; a mystery of stammers from the dramatist of stammers, Emily Dickinson—of hesitation—of nearly unspoken—unspeakable perhaps—Threats ("A sumptuous Destitution") to all that we Think we Perceive:

In many and reportless places
We feel a Joy—
Reportless, also, but sincere as Nature
Or Deity—

It comes, without a consternation—
Dissolves—the same—
But leaves a sumptuous Destitution—
Without a Name—

That is what matters! It is good to read the masters of the past in their success: Homer, Sappho, Lucretius, Virgil, Du Fu, Chaucer, Shakespeare, Dickens, Whitman, Dickinson, Rossetti

(Christina), Twain, a list I make very quickly and pretty much arbitrarily, save that, for the first six writers, we have no idea what training they had in their art, and that for the last six, we know that they had no particular training; in fact, none of them either enjoyed or tolerated much formal education at all. Each of them might as well be anonymous (efforts continue to anonymize poor Shakespeare). What they left, they left. The rest of the tradition, almost all of the tradition, belongs to the written Codex. We belong to that Codex, but only insofar as we have done the work we know and think and strive to do. For itself.

*

A. R. Ammons, an outsider writing largely in disregard of the professional inside he also belonged to, shows us as we are, in the world we most regard, from *Garbage:*

> the shapes nearest shapelessness awe us most, suggest
> the god: elemental air in a spin, counterclockwise
> for us, lets its needlepoint funnel down and gives us
>
> a rugged variety of the formless formed:

*

> and from this book's "String Theory":
> "We approach the task of listening
> through the veil of meaningless distraction."

*

We remember also and we celebrate the human need to leave the chthonic realm for the bright air. It is the human glory to soar. It is the human virtue to know where we are soaring to. We try to understand that the rational deity of reality and fate is only Gravity. We do return. We try to land soft.

Waiting for Odysseus

Eumaeus Tells a Story to Himself that Evening
in Company of Two Young Pigs

Was it Phemios I have heard tell it?
That after the first thrill of ascension
the young man Icarus began to look about, to take stock,

to take the beginning of possession, to take,
ah, breath from the source of his flight.

Near ground, he fluttered to get used to his wings.
Small brown birds fluttered back at him in their automatic mock
attack.
He bridled and sniffed at their petty affront.
Gnats to his ambition.

He ascended.
A pair of ravens in mating ritual stopped in their fertile orbit
but only to pause
and unite again to ignore his glory.

Before he ascended to the high orbit of the albatross,
the bird had not bent a wing in her perpetual glide, but flinched
now,
veered and escaped the grin of the young man's greater orbit.

It is agreed among the few that regard the sky closely
that the Phoenix ignored him entirely.

He saw and then ascended farther to race the chariot of the sun,
Helios
a distant god, rival to his ascending aspirations and

a new and worthier father,
who seemed to slow now for the young man to pass and close
in their common proximity.

*

But then, I recall the poet to say,
in a blind and golden moment the body of the young man flashed
fire,

crashed, roasted charred blood sunset-sky red,
rotted quick to mire and bone
and could not be put back together.

But the spirit of the young man, translucent as the air
he no longer breathed, but still,

both whole-figured and invisible in the light
could not ever again descend to the sacred Earth.

And the father of the young man, Daedalus,
builder unbuilded,
architect of the chthonic aurochs-realm, despaired.

And the teller concludes that, starved for the comfort of his son
and in the shame of the wild ascension of hubris,

the father ate only his despair,
and despair poisoned him until he could not
finish his dying.

Consider Tithonus.
Scan the high horizon of all who cannot finish their dying.
And taste the raw luck we simple share.

Icarus Rising

Part I

Lift

Words with Heraclitus, 1

In his errant confidence
Heraclitus declaims

Now that we can travel anywhere,
we need no longer take the poets

and myth-makers for sure witnesses
about disputed facts. (i)

*

Sitting out in the morning sun
Eumaeus scratches his dinner behind the ear

and does not say aloud:

Now that we know that however far
we travel we are in the vastness:

nowhere yet—
how can we hope to arrive without

poets and myth-makers for mused
witness among disputed facts?

Our Hands

The exactitude of execution an ancient artist
employs in the details of a bird,
titanium sheen delineated—

and yet we still have trouble depicting hands,
and hands seem not to be complex appendages.
So why?

The hand of a young woman over there by the lake
stops painting, brush in midair.
She looks beyond her brush and a wing of fingers.

She seems to look somewhere over the water.
The hand with its brush moves out beyond her attention.
Ah. That's why. The young dancer

knows her moves, watches each part of her body
work in no more than mechanical exactitude. Then
                                her left hand

                                moves by itself and
                    she follows
the grace of it.

Onomatopoetics

in memory of Hugh Fenton, grandfather
and soundsmith

"Evening,"
I just now whuspered to a young couple
and a frasky black labradory.

A good mistake, whusper,
for a worthy benediction, even
worth all your 50 most favorsome

words all by itself
and all by itsall . . . only whuspered,
for the hushed grace of breath.

*

Whuspering is like a study in musical sounds,
unabstrusive,
three bits of noise

distracted from explictation
that become sound,
as we choose to distinctguish,

notated in choreographed calligraphy
somehow to indicate
and regulate with procedure

that which is fraught

>>>

with intellectible archivity.
The cogitabund brain in tipsy labor.

*

Is it in the hapsome composition of the song
or is it in the technical tackle
by which that which was born music

is made no more than more complex?
Is it out of mire complexity that sound
and grounded art are manipufactured?

Whusper that for me, will you?
Whusper it sin technica. Sin.
Be an heated breath unheeded.

*

"Language,"
Language persuades me,
"is a democracy of sounds with its singular autonomies."

To exercise favoritism among discrete noises
is to risk appropriating a few of them above
all the others.

Such partiality chosen is to risk in turn
the insidious reaction of all the others—
a cacophonous rebellion

the ticktapping

>>>

water torchère of writer's clock,
unless some lorn whusper, longing

*

shall bow sunward,
take to the shallow peak:
paper:

a flat dis-tract, arable—
to plow in sillion, verses.
The necessary mould.

The End of Thinking

responding to some poems by Louise Glück

How hard to think.
How much harder
when you suddenly discover
that you are the rear end
of the severed worm.

Or the severed thumb
of a starfish—
and how did you know
which of the five points
was the thumb?

And even if you think
you're sure about the issue
what have the distractive
possibilities of the question done
to your treasured sense of discrete identity?

How hard to think
when you suddenly discover
that you are the front end
of the severed worm,
because you find yourself

altogether bumfuzzled
by the anatomical probability that

>>>

you should be able to miss the hinder half
more than it is able to miss you.
But you don't, can't, know.

Now, embrangled in refrangible questions,
you surrender what you might have thought
was your abiding identity to some wriggling shadow
of someone else's scattered ends of incarnation.
Poet that you are, you discover for yourself
the lachrymose end of the annelid.

Meningslöshet:

"A more solid ghost with each of those years"
for Hazel
När man kommt så långt som jag i meningslöshet
är vart ord åter interssat. (ii)
Gunnar Ekelöf

"You are a poet," she said all of a flash of a sudden.
"And you're right. You don't write in metaphor.
But you are a poet."

*

A trope that is intended to stand
in the place of something else:
as in a ratio, cannot be a metaphor.

A metaphor can only be *intended*
to seem and seeming to ask: ?

If the other side of the ratio :: (?)
intends to do more than seem
then it is false:
a schoolroom didacticism.

*

The windscape of metaphor is a way
out of a misunderstanding

>>>

by replacing it
with a misunderstanding
that a poet can live with for the time being,
which may be the time-
being of forever.

If however the next metaphor is a trap
the Old Poet will have to
wriggle himself out of it—
probably by the tentative virtue
of a new metaphor—

and the next . . . and then . . .
the reality slips
to mathematics with nor integer nor nil,
music without sound, or rest.
Or sound.

Still, trying to understand
what I am doing reinforces
with a ticklish prick of doubt
my understanding of the limits
of my diversions.

*

A metaphor
that does not deepen the mystery,
an obsidian prism,
is a stick broken from a dead branch
for you to fetch and return:

>>>

back and forth,
a harness-beast plowing out your verses.

*

Unless.
Unless the metaphor is self-generated.
Unless the metaphor *is!* and you can't help it.
Then the language is not a metaphor, but

*

the construing poet *Is*—
who speaks from the gods, especially
while the poet invents them.

Not the metaphor
but the work around it is half-
and-ill-formed to include us, the lot of us—
poor struggling contrivers who write
and our conspirators who read—

who unite to make/unmake the metaphor:

Det lilla ordet du
kanske ett glaspärla . . .
Det stora order jag
kanska et flintskärva . . . (iii)

Garter Snake Dies for Your

What it needs is a good set of wings.
Or maybe only feathers here and there.

Not for flight but for plumage.
Panache.

He may become in spectacle as God.
Not God, not deadly, but death merely

to small matters of appetite and
its own death; no more than yours or mine.

*

Bright-striped Lucifer, O my match,
show what we do not remember—

the first birth—microbe or soul forgetting
its dimensions and its sole self into life.

For any re-birth is death and unremembered
as well, so far as we remember.

So far as we know, no difference exists
in existence. Life as imagined

is only memory, building between
and toward each possible discrete exit.

>>>

Be discreet, you say, of my democratic impatience.
Discretion spreads some light on the issue:

some light on the discretion of nature,
the moral tension designed in ellipses.

Swamp Gas

1. Ignis Fatuus

Ghost lights refuse to light our way
because the way through the world
is often distracted by rough bits—
difficulties, confusions leading sometime
to the night-heron's distant shriek,

sometimes to the silent owl—
sometime-moments, or hours or longer,
incendiary occasions when the predominant
images seem down-right ugly,
shrill confusions that cramp the spine.

We must not over-refine these little dithers.
Even tarnished purity lasts,
lingers, smells, mists over
to tease the future stammering
with sensate uncertainty.

Those of us who were raised
the weedy scions of carboniferous families
share the advantage
that we are un-reared,
free of homely constraints. Without choosing,

we choose the rivers we paddle about in,

>>>

and we share the weedy smell of hubris
and decaying verdure,
ooze of potential energy,
the red-tide bubbles of reality—

outsized salamanders
born out of lightning-struck fern-trees
that reach for the dense ozone
hovering forty feet above ignition.

Newts two meters long
with sloshing eel-tails slop among swamp-edge
ferns and horsetails—
all food and fuel,

waiting out their centuries of languorous appetite
and weighted by Latin names
unfamiliar to all in the rank swank fen
but their Anthropocene descendants
in two-meter eyeglasses.

2. Will-o'-the-Wisp

A feeble muse,
Pieris rapae, Cabbage White,
flutters again out from the igniting flora,
over white-caps into the blue wind of my attention.

How many summers since last time?

>>>

Was it before the winter
my aunt Nancy looked
out her window

and saw
through our blinds closed tight
the woman in white
wintering in our empty house?

Such in-sight is the explosive propellant
of the out-wrought imagination, the
age-damaged spirit guide—

our concoction of glimmering fantasies
among the accidents of energy,
the madcap defenses
against the adventure of dotage.

Query from the Excluded Third

Nurse Kraschette frowns—
profoundly distracted.
On a scale of ***1*** to ***10***, she'd asked,
what is the level of your pain?
I asked back,
what conditions stand for the outside limits?

I cannot in courtesy stop
at this extraspective bewonderment
for an officious assessment
of all the petty pains I have felt
from birth pang and spankings
to sciatica, heel spur, gout. But—

but,
hesitation is self-serving.
On no particular scale,
I have felt less pain
than the many good people
whom I insult with my carping.

I can judge that ***1*** must be somewhere
in the neighborhood of being sensate,
waking after a lone night
on the dew of a cool summer morning,
breeze wafting gently over my whiskers
from the direction of the lake—

>>>

the sun, the day's birth.
I will surmise that ***10*** is echoed
by the penultimate gasp
or gurgle after the final
tug at the wheel of the rack.
Fine.

But what does any of that mean
in the nature of feeling?
What is the sensation before the final
pitiable gasp?
Or the appendicitis attack?
Or heat rash?

Most uncomfortable, but no. Tough,
but certainly no more than ***5***, maybe ***7***.
What feeling, on any scale,
is mere recognition of sensation—a ***1***?
Does sensation begin at a level of pain
or a level of pleasure?

Out of what bounds?
What neighborhood?
How cool or warm?
What,
on a level of ***1*** to ***10***
is that breeze if it is only wafting?

Where is the summer morning,
at what latitude or elevation?

>>>

What level of pain
is moving a fountain pen across paper,
even one held in an old
man's arthritic hand?

At what level of what pain-scale
is remembering?
What level of all levels does not,
for the sake of remembered experience,
cover the range—the Epicurean agon
of the well-lived entropy?

At the DMV

Twenty-two people standing
in line, a labyrinth of black web
from door over dull-tiled floor
eventually all the long way

to a—believe it!—friendly clerk.
It is a line made for patience,
for looking at the people around,
for reading standing, for wondering:

*

Why is it that I, the only Anglo
in this line in the neighborhood
where I will have lived with my family
for fifty years in two weeks, why—

and I share in line a slowness
of natural migration to consider—
why, the company I am almost
keeping for some of a morning,

why standing here among this
disarmingly shaded assortment
of my fellow citizens, gives me
this sensible wonder of regard?

>>>

Because, perhaps, enjoyment of
this space of morning, writing
those three brief stanzas, answers
the question I needn't have posed.

Saint Francis in Biology Class

under-and-overheard

Why intone the tedious,
well meaning, "Bless you"
when the sneeze itself is a gift,
reminding that we are here,
alive, vulnerable,
modestly shamed maybe,
momently and uncontrollably,
humanly noisy and already blessed
by and for some holy purpose:
We are charged
to evolve!

*

Two Students Observe:
"The Scorpion is
all he needs to be and
no more."
"Like Jesus?"

Maybe.
Maybe, but anyway,
all we need to be—
until we evolve

*

if we evolve?

Schubert's Second Cello

Chironomid midges in airborne shoals
find sheltered corners in corners.
Corners defined by buildings.

Corners described by angles
midges might notate, choreograph
from tree trunk to tree trunk.

Then they find corners
where there are no,
cannot be, corners,
where they swarm
to pantomime angles
in the very middle of bare air . . .

Like the violin
that slips round the corner
of the imagination
where the phantom soul
of the second of the two cellos
augurs the sad honey
of the day's climax and lorn completion.

The night though . . .

The handprint on the cave wall
prefigures nothing

>>>

but the meaning we try to give it.
Let it signify no more than its presence,
the silent adagio for what is always
about to be heard round the corner.

Like the midge, we are blessed.
Having no adequate word for "never,"
the present never ends.
One day will we somehow be compelled
to search out a meaning
for "present"?

And like the Quintet,
like the shadow of a pantomime,
like the notes left in the mind
after Schubert's final adagio,
a midge will live for no more
than the flittering shoal
of the present declining day.

A Sunday Afternoon in the Garden of Anthropos

In my garden I have entertained,
have been thrilled and calmed,
by their colors, their glamor,
by their endearing chatter—

the flights, flocks and frolics of birds,
some kinds as alien as humans
to this drag-line stripped desert,
alien as we are to each other.

Goldfinches, grackles, sparrows, doves—
mourning, white wing, Inca, collared—
birds alien as mockingbirds and starlings,

or, native to the desert, hummingbirds
and the Gila woodpecker, both
alien instead to the plastic feeder.

Once, for a few weeks,
a lone remnant quail,
silent. No kin to keen for.

*

In my workshop, my back and attention turned,
I hear now and then a whoosh of wings like a whirlwind.
The birds disappear.
.In the accident of the garden, the trees

>>>

and feeders form such comforting unity of temptation
that as I do, birds mistake garden for safety.

Just outside the cedar-plank fence
cats lurk to lunge.
Alien to everything and nothing—
cats preen.
The quail has disappeared.

I have the sense to be nervous about the garden's birds.
Nevertheless, I mostly follow
the casual appetite of feral cats.

In me, in my cognate imitation of evolution—
secure in my fenced garden,
even my breathing is omnivorous
and insatiable.

I would rather remain human: humane as I was
brought up to be, or at least pretend.
I would leave the place of ease and temptation.

I would move away from here, but
I have nowhere to go
but everywhere.

For Anthropos,
wherever is no place but
everywhere.

Some Small Thing, Tan

A tan insect
not a mosquito but tan
not so dull as the tan of the mosquito—

brighter
a little yellow in the mix perhaps.
Certainly not a mosquito

or I would be slapping
and I would have enjoyed scant guilt and scanter sorrow

in the matter because of
the customary cold wave of colder recognition:

the Mosquito—
her poisonous reputation.
But this tan with its bit of yellow, jumps

and scampers in the sun on the arm of the swing
like a hot-sand sand flea or
an electrified puppy.

We share the same sun, the same swing.
We are entertained by

the same shocks of fear and the same stunned
shocks of release.

>>>

Decide with us
while light shines on these pranks,
to share the antics of evolving.
"Yip!"

Subjective

He sees a bear,
changes the subject
to his new red-and-white speedboat.

She sees the doe with two fawns,
changes the subject to her new blue sofa,
two screen porches and
"I don't know
how many times we've moved the bed!

I want to see the sunrise
without having to move." and
"Oh, but you two are so lucky!
You see everything."

Perhaps so,
but I want to tell her somehow gently—
we see only the things we are moved to see,
and we have to get up to welcome the dawn.

We are so brightly moved
maybe only because
we cannot afford to be owned
by a subject to change to.

Icarus Rising

Common Gray

By mid-June the last trillium
displays a Lenten vigor.

Her triplet of white petals
die out to starved purple
but her energy is set in seeds.

Gray phoebe shares her usual
nesting site with us, her nest
wedged into a corner of the eave
of her shared summer cabin.

Her young are a growing pile
of brown energy fledging to
her mother's common gray.

This morning their hunger
was expressed in angry peeps,
petulant travesty of birdsong,
and we wakened to their need,
even before dawn.

We learn
to listen to our fellow residents'
children in our common hunger.

>>>

Without our futile guidance
of a withered spring metaphor
they live almost on their own.

And by tomorrow perhaps
they will have flown—with
luck and courage to survive
our perilous communal air.

Arboreal

It's in the awkward starting out
That I'm most afraid, but then
The back of my right ankle thunks
Gently against that upper branch

Beyond my head and longest reach,
And I wiggle my way up
Against the resisting bark
Until I hang from the tenderness

At the back of both my knees, rest
A minute, aim, regret the boxer shorts
Of every mother's summer regimen,
And then swing once, lurch upward

From the back swing and grab that first
Branch above the new enlightening
Pain of my abraded knee backs.
This is the only way to climb

This high in the geometry
Of this monkey-puzzling cottonwood,
But now I have the view and all
The time in my morning's world

And the time to rebuild the world
Below to the giddy standards

>>>

Of my gigantic floral growth,
And the horizon and no time

At all to wonder why, or why
I have so barked my naked legs
So fearlessly, to find this perch,
So unsoaring, sub-eagled. And then

I look through the peak of the tree
Into the branch-webbed infinity
Of sky and the next possible reach
For my searching hand.

Part II

de Aztlan, de la Frontera

Slalom tracks from last night's sidewinder,
some little drama of appetite

some kangaroo rat may have lived
to tell about or may have not,

but not to tell you and me,
stopped here in the sand wondering.

The rat is well on into the motive for his leap back
into a night that stays to enlighten only us.

The Fall of Icarus:

A note on the poet's bathetical aesthetic: Mistaking the Icarus of Breugel for the (non-existant [?]) Icarus of Dürer is the "Keatsian" mistake referred to in "Barrio Alto 2." The correction back to Breugel is the poet's way of painless atonement. The addition of Diego Rivera seems appropriate to the issues of the sequence.

Eumaeus Old and the Magpie

I thought I saw a magpie.
Came out of a pine tree.
Black and white.

What other bird
might be hereabouts
that is black and white?

I think it was black and white.
It was that fast, and the forest so thick.
Like the rest of life.

I would fly off with the black and white bird.
I would fly off with the bird that is not
black and white. That never was.

I would fly off with a bird of no color.
I would fly off with no color.

>>>

No bird.

Old age brings passive recklessness.
I ignore the name of my pilot.
Aiee Karos he seems to declare through his flames.

So he is a magpie, after all.
Brash ash-and-charcoal.
Good company for a wagtongue's waning days.

I. Barrio Alto 1

Colonia Microondas, Guaymas, Sonora, Mexico
outside La Iglesia de Santa Maria de los Angeles,
known as "La Portiuncula"

José Pedro hangs around the mission this morning.
This morning again.
This morning is almost always the same morning.

Like almost always
José Pedro won't earn any money again.
No job again this morning.

Like almost always
José Pedro will climb back up the steep hill
back to his colonia in the barrio.

José Pedro will take the little pail
of watery beans and rice from the mesón Franciscana
back up the dusty steep hill to his plywood chabola

like almost always and then like almost always
he will take his broom up on his shoulder
and he will walk along the saddle of his hill.

He will walk to the little open-air chapel,
La Portiuncula,
and he will sweep the day's dust from the concrete floor.
Then he will lean on the broom,

>>>

his vertical *prie-dieu* now,
and he will look out over the bahía far below.

He might imagine the blue sea vastly beyond.
He will approve the hard grace of cardón-blessed
desert mountains, like almost always.

Then he will maybe lean toward me
as though I were really there and he will remind me.
Es bonito he will breathe

like almost always.
Always
something is beautiful.

II. Las Golondrinas

Colonia Ranchito, Guaymas, Sonora, Mexico

In the age when they were all taught
the touch of fingers and hands on cool Earth,
to caress smooth clay,
to shape slick mud
into purpose and beauty,

the clay was their teacher,
their cool wet guide to the next shape,
their lesson in clear judgment—

the purgatory of the kiln
in which the clay died a death
they could grieve wholly in sadness and love.

The kiln—the sunstone that grows too hot,
too bright not to remind us of some distant power
in the great dark cosmos—
dimensions of gravity,

because it is the sun's daily job to be where it is,
placed in orbital inexactitude like
the circle of creosote bush,
a monument to the sun that grew
like a giant's fairy ring

in which enchanted dancers
chanted paeans to the sun long before,

>>>

millennia before I picked
up this shard of old pottery,
the one in my hand with most
of a purple blossom fading

or the piece of green bottle glass,
washed by so many of the so infrequent rains
that its cutting edges
are only as rough now as working hands
to my investigating touristical soft fingers

that touch the dry air in the direction
of the children
on the edge of the arroyo,
who stare at me ready to smile again.

I will wave.
I will pick up a bit of old pitcher,
part of its lip still attached.

The flowers on it are yellow
under scratched glaze.
I wave again.
Children wave back.

I have forgotten to bring candy.

That matters.
But they wave back anyway.
That matters,

>>>

to all of us, much more.

*

That is a scallop shell,
lying on the pink sand beside a wine bottle bottom,
symbol and tool of centuries of pilgrims,

Las Golondrinas,
las peregrinas descalzas, turning,
returning, turning,
like centuries of furrows of unshod poems.

Candyless, the children wave some more,
all pilgrims,
they from their plywood chabolas,
me from somewhere north,
seductive treacherous El Norte.
They know.

They are children, at home.
They expect to offer their smiles,
and not for candy, only—
for the return of inexpressible sentiment.

My being here pleases them more than it pleases me,
so I must suppose, but
no.

It pleases el norteño in me less than me myself.
Even I am almost elated now—
at home for a moment and shy as the children.

>>>

I ask if I can keep the bits and pieces.
The children smile and wave,
Las Golondrinas also,
like me in the moment,
Las Golondrinas del Pobrecillo.

Someone, who only might have been me,
or anyone else,
has offered them something they can give back.

*

Junk matters here, or the many colors of junk,
the broken elements of such permission
as they are blessed to offer.

An old saguaro stands sentinel in the sun.
It will stand almost as long as the junk I leave behind.

Las Golondrinas will fly away
when they sense food somewhere else,
and return to the barrio.

Or they will flop broken winged here in the dump
with the many broken flowers, desiccating
amid the fractured beauty of shards,
all that remain of their artful touch—
their broken tears.

III. In Security Malignant

1

Inside—its open structure—
the little church in Colonia Microöndas:
light—desert light, searing,
a comforting threat
as perilous as fate, but
safer by far than the brute machinations
of human ideologies.

Outside, Josué doesn't smile,
the child behind the fence rails,
small boy whose face fills some part
of me with a caul of some basic memory
of my own face,
unsmiling and perfectly—no—
something like
but not really
happy.

Inside, light chooses to emit itself
through yellow-tinted—
maybe plastic-paned—
windows high above the pews,
chosen perhaps because this off-color
was available somewhere nearby
and affordable in a barrio mercado.

Maybe. An accident of something

>>>

resembling but, providentially?,
not gold.
Light!

Desert noon light,
neither yellow nor gold,
but which may become either
in the internal silence of aftermath.

*

Is the boy happy? Happenstance:
a property of grace
suspended in a time of suspicion and
incivil forced dispersion.

Behind the little iron railing outside,
almost as open as the church itself,
Josué stands, looking out, through,
into unrestricted life around him—

his family, people talking,
Sunday dinners being planned,
even the traffic moving
gently among the Sunday gathering
of the boy's family and nearest neighbors.

He looks through the fence rails,
the boy who needn't smile.
From the lawn, distracted from a pleasant
late Sunday morning chat,
I look through the rails—

>>>

wrought iron
decorated at the top of each rail
with a black acorn I think, or pineapple—
something innocent, menacing—
petty decorations fading.

*

I look through the rails.
For a minute or two, without moving,
I approach Josué
whose unsmiling face is a glory of our degraded peace

and as I approach without approaching
the fence decorations recede
into some ether beyond my narrowing range of sight,
and the rails close in on his face and on my eyes.

The rails thicken as I get near—
or the nearing of those rails toward me—
and thicken.
They thicken, I see, say, into bars

thick, black, corroded
like the two faces in the poem
that dissolve with the poem
behind the malignant smear of bars

*

of wall.

*

>>>

So the border closes once more,
and once more I cannot decide
which side I want to live on.

*

Returned to Arizona
through dispatriating gestures
at the alien border of the alienating nation I was born to,
I think back, see back to the face of the boy.

I know which side.
I want to live on the side where the most living happens.
I want to live on any side without a border.
Without a wall:

Sin borde.
Sin pared—

because:

2
after Profound Concentration,

this slick arrogance spread
across the marble floors of legal pages
might slide like fragile plates, not

that purposeful grace of outer magma,
our volcanic firmament
so innocent of violent intent

>>>

but only the inept intent and *entente* of leadership,
all smiles, all power riding easy
on ample loins

slumming far from admissible distance
outside their zoological display of distrained childhood—
fear-bound ground in cages,

no promise or hint of emancipation—
only dry wind from hired functionaries,
an *apparat* of withered mouths.

Institutions, like
governments ungoverned,
living only to perpetuate *terminus ad quem*,

must rot to the skeletons of nothing
but themselves having gained no flesh
but only the smell of dead ideals

sizzling on ignited covenants—
the stench of deceit, the dust-fragrance—
far-distant obliviated life

by rude calculation mis-engineered—
the *memento mori* of each child's breath
publicly disdained—in the ignoble country

where I choose not to avoid living
and where I expect to breathe out my own living
publicly disdained in my turn.

Envoi, Opuntia

Cactus blossoms, waxy yellow profusion
of prickly pear on the bajada,
purple blossoms of staghorn,
smell from a polite distance, subtly sweet.

Approach slowly until you sense the fragrance.
Then stop.
Stay where you are and let your nose work
without your brainish interference. It is

a subtle fragrance, but not if you get too close, if you
stick your nose where it is only the business
of bees, of bats to go.
Rare on Earth, short-lived,

cactus blossoms appeal to your modesty,
so if you have none,
gather your wealth.
Reap power. These

passing fragrances are not for you.

IV. Barrio Alto 2

On the wind-scourged top
of a steep rock-strewn saddle
the crowded chabolas of the poorest
of the poor in the barrio—
Colonia Proletaria on high—

blown dust burns into exposed arms,
faces turn in awe and dismay
from the 360 degree land/seascape,
a billion-dollar view in the States.

But to be wealthy here is
to be close to the action or the ocean.
The action will never be on hilltops,
out of eyeshot, forgotten,
wall-less, exposed, bent.
and much too close
to the wind-cursed sun.

To open one's eyes from the dead soil of this hill,
is to open them onto a view of mountain and sea
that is a majesty of God's savage scathing
desert world.

The legend-scalding bahía.
See there?
Dürer's Icarus, white legs up,
his heron-wings sunk already and forgotten,

>>>

limned for a second in the polluted bay.

José Pedro sweeping the open chapel
will come to you again gently,
like the last time,
seeking work, a handout, shared words—
especially shared words.

Happily chattering without listening or seeing,
you passed so blithely
their wretched and holy chabolas
so close to heaven.

Go back and remind José Pedro
what he just said,
reminding you too—"Es bonito."
"Si, es muy bonito. Es hermoso."

On the way down the hill,
call to your better mind
the squalor of the northward crossing into Nogales—
to home.
Recall that you also
don't feel welcome there anymore.

V. The Poor of Aztlan

(The barrio, Guaymas, Sonora, Mexico)

1

Toward the north
across the border and into the desert
lives are husked by the hundreds.
Discarded bones.
Weathered carapaces
of empty gear and empty hope:

2

In the barrio children beam and pass quickly
in fresh T-shirts and stiff new jeans
on their way to the serious
business of escuela—
of living—
carry heavy backpacks.
They half skip anyway
bathed in smiles, share *Buenos dias.*

An old man sweeps
the sidewalk in front of his casa,
then about six feet into the street.
He and his home are no more than part of his barrio.
No less.

Another, younger man stands stately by this morning too.
Repeats ritual *Buenos dias,*

>>>

solemnly in desolate good humor.

Last night he had leaned against
a battered white van in front,
another borracho lost in a vaguely expectant
fuzz of alcohol.
This morning he is a neighbor again.

The little ones keep walking by,
some mothers accompanying hand in hand or from behind
not quite willing to keep up
with sillier energies.

3

Delfina stands in front of her tiny shack.
Almost a child, too slim,
mother of four—
knocked up at thirteen
and not worth a statistic.

Her chabola proclaims her future.
She hasn't one.
Delfina smiles. Waves. *Buenos días.*

4.

To the west, in the shallows off the beach at San Carlos—
dolphins, catlike, graceful,
caress swimmers' legs.

A dolphin bumps one swimmer gently,

>>>

firmly in the belly
as though to warn him against the final reality.

In our distant mythologies
dolphins rejoice to human presence.

Dolphin: from Greek, *delphus*: womb—
"We are mothers when we carry him
in our heart and body through love"—

or does the dolphin reject now the invasive species,
the dolphin's unrequited?

5

Back there in the bahía though,
where a sewage pipe slops into the dubious clarity,
and a fish processing plant and a paper factory—
stench times three,
industry pays,
and reeks.

6

The poet's Keatsian blunder:
it's Bruegel's Icarus, not Dürer's,
but the same pasty legs
whitening leprous
in the blistering stolen air above
Cortez's seething blood-corrupted sea,
matted wings on the bottom now—
ancient muck and modern oil-dreck.

>>>

7

The poet's place is the delusional mist
on the near outside of the canvas,
helpless in the fogs of language and memory—
mal-focusing lost realities,
bent histories:

The treacherous North. *Buenas noches.*

VI. Dead Beckoning

Iglesias,
vegetación de cúpulas,
sus fachadas
petrificados jardines de símblos. (iv)

Shall it be Rivera's Icarus this yarn around?
Never mind.
The image remains true—faceless,
requiteless panic insinuated in those leprous-white legs
dangling upward into some alien gravity,
down/up-and-netherward/
etherward

far beyond the care or awareness
of the women on shore,
inland and hidden in a clear field of focus
from the meta-reality
of procedural art and artists.

It doesn't matter anyway, much,
save a little perhaps to Rivera,
and certainly to me,
but mostly to the greater image, the peripheral
real world:

In a side-chapel disguised as poverty
three aged women in black,
devout lay-ordinary products of church, chapel,

>>>

compliments of sacraments—
visions and revisions of the centuries' *ad hoc* Trinities—
the women of the Trinities,
their lives invisible in the picture,
the poem, the plaster santo,
his leprous-white face:
themselves—posed like fates—

Moirai—or, perhaps:
Charites—Gratiae.

*

Blessed or cursed in a robotic vida fantasma
the painted santo raises his plaster right hand
to offer an un-live blessing
to the blind and distant noumenon

in the vacuum that surrounds
the three women in black:
they, their rosaries,
their plaster silence.

Tock Tick Tock Tick

Blessed or cursed in a Purgatory's
indifferent share of Eternity,
a time-bound proximity of novena
times novena,
times the product

>>>

of all novenas that equal the second
before the next-to-final resurrection,

a somber triad of ageless women in black
share silent histories in absentia:
a nether-cosmos, in wisdom
indifferent to the Greek logophilia.

Three ageless women in black
who have replaced
three ageless women in black
who have replaced generations
in a zodiac of ageless
indistinguishable trines in black,

sit silent,
like Moirai at their profound work,
Clotho, Lachesis, Atropos—
a black trinity arranged
before the supine effigy of a petrified santo,

who lies for the convenient ortho-dogma
of pliable theology,
which re-presents:
Is? IS!—AM!—

First Person re-manufactured Plural,
the officially apportioned
totality of the sacred One:
and Two in One: and Three in One:

>>>

and All in One: and One in three:
AM:

ALL: ANY?

*

Todo lo que tiene luz tiene sombra.
La luz y la sombra van de la mano.

Pero, si la llama misma no tiene sombra,
¿De veras tiene luz la llama de la vela? (v)

Someone's elders invented
their bound and binding character,
who evolved by prolepsis
through clinamen to prolepsis,
adventuring into their impeccably
disarranged quantum deity;

uncontrollable,
the same God who then invented time
to keep track of Himself.

Then someone
in some forgotten monastery
discovered the sear that would control
the clock that controlled time
that controlled God
and someone later re-invented God
as the Original Deists' Deity—

>>>

agreeable, sensible,
ruthless at composed formal request,
nonpræsens, nonpotentes
for all the scholastic glamour—

and immersed Him into a petrified maelstrom
in the sea far deeper than the gentle eddy
Lucretius swirled for the livelier
ancient pagan god-gang.

Du söker i de eviga det rimliga? (vi)
 Och jag?

*

The santo's stiff right arm,
a thing of wheels and cogs and metal joints,
the engineering of a drawbridge,
a ruthless angle of ascent,
a pitiless drop,

moves—tick—
heavenward from his side—
uptick and downtick,
downtick and uptick—
ticker tape listing of quantifiable prayers
or a metronome for bland eternity,

timing of a sacred doomsday clock—
to wind down some-aeon—
imperceptible though,
as though to Tithonus' deathless flagging ear,

>>>

listening in timeworn apathy

to the twittering machine,
chattering sticks upon a coat,
its tattered chords of a cactus wren
rasping dire complexities—

eternity in the endless humility of rosary beads:
like neutrinos,
omni-directed directionless
dash and flash of reckless faith.

Jag söker i ett timligt det orimliga.
Och du?

One pale stiff finger beckons
with no motion of its own,
beckons in the tick-tock tempo
that the mechanized arm in lithic pallor
directs in the evening shadow
that shrouds and portends
the final unwinding.

*

Eternity itself
arranges to beckon in time with the women's
semi-animated dead-beckoning saint.

Right arm tick.
Right arm tock.

>>>

Then tick, then tock,
half-paddling, treading desert air against
the gurgling undulations of generations
of the tocking dead—

the living,
        the dead,
                the living,
        the dead.

The . . .
The dead:
the holy dying:
the holier dead queued breathless-tight
for resurrection.

Candidates for contractual
immortality

                Matins

        Compline   Lauds

Vespers   Prime

        Nones   Terce

                 Sext:

        in hora mortis nostrae:

>>>

Tick
Wind>

Change threesome from Moirai
to Eumenides?

La enterraron en la tumba familiar
y en las profundidades tembló e polvo
del que fue su marido:
la alegría
de los vivos
es la pena de los muertos. (vii)

Check tick check TOCK.
Wind.
Watch arm TOCK

tock tick tock . . .
tock tock tock :
*

The women in black know the range of liturgies:
They are mothers.
They are grandmothers.

They represent the generations
that marry young in white—
from Quinseañera to altar in a quick-change of finery,

from white to white

to black.

>>>

They have tamed husbands—mostly tame—
and mostly for their only protection
in the earthy fields and kitchens,
the door-yards of Purgatory.

They have raised children well beyond the number
that straitens ease and maybe love—
stretched out and far away
into the population of generations
filling barrio and church
and church-yard.

The women in black
are acquainted with Earth—
the matters of nature, nurture, culture.
Death.

They are the clay! . . .
Daughters of Martha, the holy mother of nurture:
Demeter, Chthonic Mother,
ravenous to feed the living!

*

Outside the eucharistical numbness of eternality
beyond the automatic sacrifice of meditation
the women survive,
each like Persephone
caught between the god and grace.

como los sagrados emblemos profanos
of all who survive:

>>>

ellos sobriviven,

La Muerte no es más que justicia—ciega.
No menos. Pero ciega.

From the hidden spaces we share, they beckon:

> *"Don't be ashamed to be human, be proud!*
> *Inside you, vault behind vault opens endlessly.*
> *You'll never be complete, and that's how it should be."* (viii)

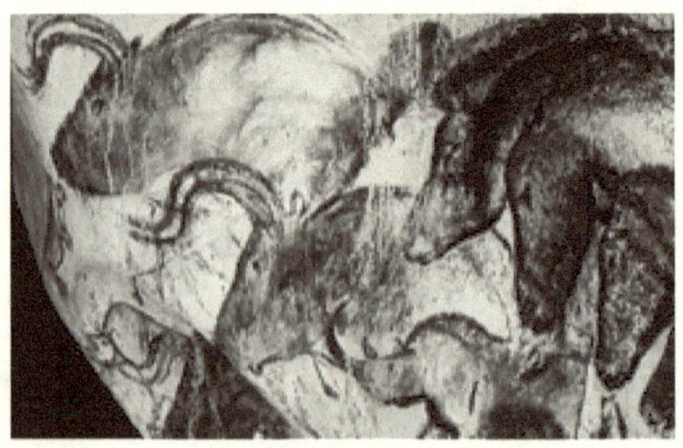

Coda: The Lady of the Pomegranate

for Carol, who keeps the plant alive.
Shelter in place, travel in Shelter—
April, 2020

Outside under any shade,
patchwork shadows of mesquite,
palo verde or sweet acacia,
deep shade of citrus,
narrow shadows of saquaro and cardón,
arms spread to the seething sky,
spine ceiling of cholla—

the temperature has risen
to a hundred and twenty degrees but
inside, the primitive efficiency of swamp cooler
forces the temperature down to seventy-eight
so long as the prosthesis of electricity holds out.

So I will not take my body outside
but to live I will send my arid soul out.
To live, my soul in turn takes me to Earth
past the lizard's crawl-space of cholla
under the healing mystery of creosote bush
and down that narrow hole,

the downward paradise of rattler,
scorpion, tarantula, Teiresias,
down under the sea of baked desert pavement
beneath the concrete of caliche,

>>>

down through the magma-cooling unguent of aquifer
until I meet the lady of the pomegranate.

She breaks open the leather of the fruit,
places a single sweet wet bead between my lips,
then another
then another
and with each seed I grow that much cooler
that much warmer.

So cool my lips
So warm her touch
Such pure sanity of shelter down
down

freed from the restraint of soul
almost ready to return to Earth—
root, branch, thorn, and oh, saguaro's
white blossom, cereus' lure of fecundity,
bats marrying cactus to cactus
in the palpitating heat of the new desert night.

VII. Awakening: a Breath of Evolution

I see no reason why purgatory
may not be reincarnation.
Denise Levertov, "A Heresy"

This bacterial volcano
raging so close to my innermost bowel
that all other worries are routed,
the scavenging lives
I have brought from innocent Mexico,
commune with me and my pain.

Together we sing in praise of mutation—
the cancer, the wart
or the mere intrusive blemishes
on ordinary old age
warm in that embrace of my flesh.

We sing
not of the pleasant metaphor of penance,
but of the thing
gestating, living,
breeding within me,
the elegance of a cell's iteration.

Then maybe I consider
in calm moments before this beauty
finally silences time—
before the community of cancer

>>>

or the zombie-life of virus
or some duplicitous fungus
survives the struggle—

that I have been this colony all along,
each cell immortal with all the rest of creation,
only the foreigners,
mind and pride
rising in their moment of untimeliness
above the evolution of the microbe,
perfect unit of my first cell.

Incarnation!

The final oneness
before the last breaking apart into a New
World of particulate independence—
protein freed to Earth or
ash to the cosmos.

My first wiggle into purgatory—
a hydra
each cell open
to every pulse of the great adventure

or a worm in the primaeval sludge,
one brave end budding into shell
then claws, scales, hair, fingernail,
the colony of primordial artists
gathered to roil a sea of rebellious ideas

>>>

to serve purgation again and again
with the colony of true creation—
fresh integrity
from that first bacterium.

Some declare that cellular life is immortality
dividing from beginning to beginning
to beginning

always in comforting symbiosis, dying
into the pastel purgatory of flesh
rebirthing us all from the first,
the last animacular farewell—

the comforting awareness
that even eternity
as we have always known in the gut,

is no more
than a single molecular step from absolute
nothing—
almost breath:
elohim.

VIII. Aliento

We were on our way out, me,
the inexcusable draft of a stalled poem—
the woman who
in what context I do not remember
nor need to know,
said the word.

The other was the word she said—

"Golondrinas,"
the word we casually asked into the car with us.

"It means 'Swallows'," she said,
and I think she explained why she said it.
I think,
but I drove away from the meaning,

and I think I will never know,
because *Golondrinas* became the *ruah*,
the imperceptible rush of wings,
the still small axis

that took over from me, and
while I had nothing more to do
with writing my poem
or do with my mind than drive,
became the voice, not mine,

>>>

but the voice of the poem,
of the birds,
of the children in the poem,
propelled on the flashing wings of the swallows,
and their own unstable plumage.

And I can become and remain
the still small
shadow of invisible Elijah.
A swallow shadow,
and the passing silent voice of
the returning Golondrinas,

or the children themselves,
an axial whisper, a swallow's down
of quick and quickly passing truth.

IX. Flores y Cantos for José Pedro

A flurry of light noises,
those bright paper flowers
we search for in fiesta markets,
or a cereus' one-night blossoms.

"Bienvenidos," and "Mucho gusto."

I had never been blessed with these sounds before.
I turned from this new music
and absorbed the shock of embrace

almost before I saw the swarthy hand I had taken,
worn both rough and smooth
by labor and idleness.

I faced him not face to face but cheek to cheek,
not the gringo way:
flowering is never to be questioned.

These blossoms never last for the answer.

By now, after our several years,
after blossoms of minutes fading
with the folklorico fiesta dye
of our minor occasions,
our minutes in hour-bound years as friends,

I still enjoy long talks with you, amigo,

>>>

separated now by distance,
time, language, and—
it's been so long ago—
maybe life.

I still absorb your spoken world
from what I can grasp—

“Es bonita,” and you gesture
beyond the adobe and plywood chabolas
toward the bay,
from that hill worth those billions
in the unfathomable attraction of the
implacable Norte—

but, we must agree again,
only after your shacks
and your children and your lives
have been sanitized away
from the gilded hills.

I smile and nod and make noises in English.
O, yes, si, beautiful, bonita,
the point and counterpoint of this dance
you and I step to, hermano,

fingertipping those paper flowers,
whose names,
all those breeze-blown words,
flores y cantos,

>>>

have wilted,

have strewn this fertile pollen,
this sometime comfortably mortal faith,
these blossoms,
with each new overture,
the two dancers we are each time.

We become pollen, tune,
flor y canto.
Embrace and change are our only,
our best language,
flower and song.

Part III

Failing Apogee

I write my name
onto the inner fly of my book.
A silly habit.
It is my signature,
illegible to any stranger
illegible to those who know me,
and know the book,
mostly illegible to me.

I do it so that the book
might read it, should the book so choose,
that the book and I have
more than a single name
to share in secret,
a sign together
of our immediate interest,
an emblem of our conversation.

Words with Heraclitus, 2

Heraclitus:

The soul is undiscovered
though explored forever
to a depth beyond report—

Eumaeus:

while the poet's words
explore breath by breath to
report beyond depth.

Once he'd got there, Heraclitus
claimed that you can't get there
*from here—*you.

But that's neither here
nor there
since we're almost always
either in one place
or another

always in one time
or another
or always all ways
and any
where.

Choose

“We need to be able to choose
our battles,” said the leader
of people devoted to non-

violence—a tenet we adopt
in order to contain the base
violence we abhor when

we employ the *non* that we,
well, abhor in our fashion too.
So, in non-battling we order

the prescribed silver chalices,
but we pay just a bit more
for the ones that look,

by an accident of peaceful
indiscretion, like patterned
steel, the design of swords.

Except Poverty

You will keep telling me that true poverty is not that.
Not living with nothing.
True poverty is solely an issue of the soul.

I got that. "The poor in spirit."
Poverty is living as *though* we were poor.
Poverty is the willingness to give it all up,
without giving up our credit cards.

Sine proprio means to live without *owning* but
not without having.
It all has to do with surplus and our little compromises
between sharing and idle discomfort.

But naked Francis on his dying-ground is naked.
Unshod Francis walking over no man's land
to chat with the Sultan *is* unshod,

and the hot desert sand is hot,
and those sharp stones are sharp.
If Francis slips on the hot sharp stones, the blood is blood.

The nails driven through Yeshua's hands and feet are nails,
and pain is almost as near eternal as doubt, as passion.

Francis never gave the spirit of anything away.
Francis gave it *all* away. Except poverty.

Icarus Rising

Stultus Dei

He sits, shoulders
foursquare and solid,
feet spread firmly sure
on the concrete
without which solemnity of human touch
perhaps this slick
arrogance of pavement

might slide like fragile tectonic plates
from its assigned place
of base utility above our
liquifacting desert Earth.

He sits erect
atop his ruptured suitcase,
by presence and sign blessing us
despite our natural misattention,
against the burn of our ultimate slide
beneath the melting asphalt.

He stretches his arms
with a messianic grace toward the sun it seems,
maybe only to shield his eyes
and ours from that sphere,
the magma we orbit, our
ultimate volcanic firmament.

He gestures, not wildly.

>>>

With passing grace,
he caresses the sky.
This is no brain-fried wilderness prophet, but

God's jongleur, another Francis,
and fortuitously no doubt,
he composes a gentle
show of harmony within himself,
for us, and we

who stop for the grace of his ceremony
merely at the cold
invitation of a traffic light,
are soothed into his gentle control
as he conducts the music of this busyness.

He gathers the air itself,
embraced in those graceful arms,
into his beauty,
composes an ordered music
from the disharmony of traffic

and thus becomes the fleeting
pantomime of a savior
in our gas-fired universe
of any who chance to stop for him.

Changing Light

A hummingbird, iridescent in green
only a few seconds ago, terrified

now, a matte flutter of black ash
in the shadows of speeding commuters,
trapped between parallels of traffic.

The bird whips in panic, spins a gray haze of wing
against the lethal human fate of servitude
to these lines of mechanized dull infinity.

Tiring, she sacrifices this constant of
geometrical absurdity for the sureness
even of the pavement she struggles from also.

The bird accepts the finality of life
as though a sure death,
even so black and foreign as this one,

serves life better than bland eternity,
fulfills the blind promise that lives in the egg.

In the Least Air

1

This hard park bench by the lakeside
offers me somehow to think of Elijah.
It is his only quiet moment, perhaps,

when he hears what the English Bible
translates the word *ruah* into that is all we know,
or maybe all we want to know—

sitting on a park bench watching
a mother mallard exercise her heron-
tempting brood of puff-balls—

all we want to know of being.
The still small voice,
the smallest emotion of moving air.

We watch ducklings, paddling puff-balls,
and we consider the heron, hunting silently
in the early summer reeds.

We anticipate the pike, skulking his way
through the dank of cabbage weeds. We
anticipate fear with such a quiet gasp

that only the down on the smallest
molecule can feel our breath.

>>>

2

At a picnic table nearby

a quiet violence of dispute:
"This isn't your table.
We don't have anything for you. Get away."

The ragged girl looks at him and asks,
"Aren't even the dogs given scraps
from the picnic basket?"

Then he sits with her, and I cannot hear the down
of his breath of apology.
They eat, and they feed the circling dogs.

String Theory

1

The still small voice barely breathes.
We approach the task of listening
through the veil of meaningful distraction,
of idle talk of this or that,
exercises of the tongue, or of sleep—
purposeful dreams.

All is respiration,
tug and warp of original
inspiration, the constant movement.
The final medium,
the knowledge of what is heard
of this news of death.

The still sculpture,
bare skull, sullied flesh,
is mere expiration,
waste of breath and spirit,
the soundless voice, subatomic truth
blown away with desert sand.

It is an urn fired dead,
a petrifaction of spirit,
rock-bound, sere,
if only to invite us into the saving
confusion of life—
distractions, dappled,

>>>

malleable, breathing—
the being of it all.

2

This being,
undiscovered identity
behind the original atomic mote—
one neutrino, or wave, or string
away from infinity
in the vastness of our single miniscule
universe among the infinitude
of all possible universes,
the isness of it all.

If I stoop to calculate,
step my bare-foot way out of Eden
unpropelled by awe,
I have not fallen, nor can I.
The photograph does rob from the soul,
and calculation is mere photography.

The true physics is still all dream,
palpable until dawn,
soaring nevertheless at light-speed to escape
the flick of the shutter,
the switch on the blank wall
that turns life into artifact.
It is our incalculable physics
of dream and story.

Chuang Tzu's Monkeys

"This animal advertised his own cleverness.
He thought no one could touch him." (ix)

1 *(1965)*
Formless gray bug fumbles
into a corner of my eyeshot.
I two-hand swat it
for its mosquito pretension.

Some admonition might
Zhuangzi give here
casually to ward off
disaster to the ambitious,

from the shadow now
of his westering way,
the crumpled silk
of his small fame.

2
Will the next monkey
to read Master Zhuang learn?
No. He will be hired
as a prodigy to perform,

reading loudly to masses
who will destroy him
in their envy, their

>>>

formaldehyde admiration.

3 (1995)
A trophy fish,
perfected in plastic
but surely not its old
self, hangs high,

proud on a suburban wall,
admired for size,
shades of color,
poise of attack stroke,

is nevertheless dead
for the beauty endowed it.
Zhuangzi, poet of no size,
but shades of color,

poise of no attack, hangs
nailed to the trophy wall
of my molded, shaded,
buoyant, polystyrene

notions, all spaced
in bucolic clutter.
And my own
raw monkey-pelt?

>>>

4 *(2015)*
In my way I follow
the master's indirection,
avoid intent.
Pelt stretched here, wrinkled there,

balding and baggy-eyed,
I have subtly avoided
the eight by ten glossy
by way of the program

of unstudied inaction.
But what about legacy?
Ah. Styles change. What
does the man of summer Dao

know about the great world's
taste in the demimonde
of monkeys? Only,
how to avoid that tree.

5 (2020)
Tree?

Bottom Dwelling

The bottom
of this lake
is a house
of gray—

made so
by the flick
of the fish's
tail

after he chooses
to rise
to the agony
of color

writhing
inches below
the kaleidic
surface.

And the gray
is cold
and constant—
secure

where we
choose to stay

>>>

with the memory
of our

bright joys
and never
dare flick
our own tails

to rise above
the pregnant
shroud
of mud

For the Primary Percent

and Those They Elect to Power

1

The virus is a creature,
for the virus is created—
by its host if by no god.

The virus is talented.
The virus cheats life
by being half life

and all death:

2

like you maybe
in your viral urge
to devour all

that is creative, all
that is productive
in the world.

Half life
and all
death—

and an unworthy insult
to the honest skill of the
industrious virus.

Part IV

Failing Wings

Comment

Eumaeus, lend me a moment of your silence.

Scratch a piglet behind the ear and smile
for the trio of us. For the most distant of us

is sorely without master or morale.

I admit to an impulse in this sequence that calls me to remind
the old poets, Eumaeus, and me, and some others slinking about,

of the dangers and of the inevitable futility of writing topical
poems.
The most futile danger is in presuming that topical literature is
literature.

The sense of futility comes in the understanding that, Ezra's
wisdom
notwithstanding, most "news that stays news" remains nothing
but news,

like the catalog of Argive ships before Troy or the Charge of the
Light Brigade,
empty shadows of occasions that remind us nevertheless

to wave at the clouds of shadow with a will to understand
what they seem to obscure, if only the folly of glory and the glory
of folly.

Still, parlous times call for some sacrifice, to help ward
off the ultimate futility with present utility.

We Are Wired into the Currents

The petty seep of violence
that will come burbling
back again up-stream
like Cosmoline on water—

*

I need to know what else
beside the elation of love
and the fulfillment of grief
takes us so far beyond

the simple current of our primordial wiring—
ears maybe to listen to the sonic eclipse
between the quail's murmur
and the dove's keen.

Nor do they, the quail, the dove, the sound,
the silence, need me to make more of them, or less,
and they are themselves only to themselves—
hapful fabrication only to me.

Unmoving brown/gray keepers of nature's lowly
wisdom—their sounds illuminate my eyes!
more still by far than our dead moon's stare,
and I make conversation that only we can share.

*

>>>

In the threat of darkening near distance,
from the direction of a white birch
bent over the lapped shore
we hear night herons shrilly drooling.

Failing Wings

near Nevada, Iowa

Puddle from the storm just past.
Fecund mud quivering into clover,
young tender thistles learning to grasp.

Dim clinging memory avoids the inevitable spreading heat,
drought from fearsome altered skies, drought
from a gilded cradle of leadership in dotage

and also losers, like
a redwing blackbird we see
perched for the brief moment of his flute solo.

The bird sits on a barbed-wire fence,
enforced separation—a wall of strands—
at the dry edge of a green sward,

bucolic interlude between West Indian Creek
and the soybean farm plowed under this summer,
for sale to some underbidding conglomerate next year.

Blackbird pays his hungry attention,
such attention as he allows
to human pretension—

to a plowed crop of new debt instantly forgotten
by the great one who nevertheless loves his farmers

>>>

momently from and between his stroppy nation's mental lapses,

practiced, unpracticed, practiced, dispracticed—
the tutored praxis of a senile megalomaniac and boor,
Peter's pumpkin in a gilded palace.

The DTs*

(pretending to be 1965 again; pretending
to be stuck in the elevator at a prominent
New York publishing house: dreaming)

Isolate I,
becalmed in an elevator,
dangling in peace and trepidation

above a gentle netherworld,
the nether-basement below me,
immune to up and down but yo-

yo-ing now dreamwise sideways,
timeward, fated against
an evening of literate companionship,

of wit, and one, two or,
well,
maybe just one more.

No, scotch, rocks,
a little water,
not so much . . .

Desires jugged in an elevator between the sanctity of and the
pro-
fessional word-hoard where I had planned carefully not to get off.
My righteous thirst for the unsullied Plaza Hotel—

>>>

blesséd years before the thumping and harrumphing and garrumphing, years hungry now for-all-and-nothing, fuming, fumbling, fee-fie-foe-fumming, trumpety-trum-trum-Trumpeting.

Trumpetless of fanfare in the days of peace and the light blanket
of darkness birthed and blessed by no more than
a gentle ephemeral blackout that threatened then no more than a
silly moment of fortunate eternity—
in the days before the newest exile of the Black, of Brown, of
Women, of Poor, of Sane, of Educated, of *etc, etc, etc,*

all the many faceless *etceteras,*
the *et alii,*
the you and the me and each anonymous pronoun.

Our ninety-nine percent dreary off-the-rack otherness—
All, All!
"Out!"

In the time-free elevator is peace still,
gliding nohow in gentle protection,
locked free in a concrete empyrean—

of a fairy tower,
all time jugged together now, while . . .
Outside? . . .

Oh, our delirious endtime!

*No. No, not those DTs. The elected and
its minions. Pretty much the same, though.

Entr'acte—Bait: A Fable of 2020

So it's this frog, don't you see, and he's fishing,
just lying back in his old boat against this log
that he's got for a front seat, and he's not thinking
at all, just like anyone who's fishing,

and mostly finding just the right place
in the small of his back to rest against that log.
Just fishing, like I say, when he sees that
while he wasn't paying attention, his own bait,

this big perch minnow, has taken hold of his own
webby foot and is eating its way up his tasty left leg,
when the frog remembers that *he* is *a frog!*
for gosh sakes, and that's when Truth

starts eating at him too, and he thinks:
When I'm just sitting and doing nothing
but watching the bobber do nothing too,
sometimes the Big Answers come to me anyway:

like, one way or another, whether we're princes
or frogs, we all wind up nothing but bait.
But by the time he's finished with his very short
period of first time thinking,

and the perch has worked his way up to the frog's

>>>

fishing vest, that hooked minnow has proved
the point for both of them,
                                    and me too, I guess,
when I look down to check out what's left.

Earth-Bound, Moon-Mad

We travel from Third World state through
Third World state, eight of them this trip,
all wards of the Federal CCC.*

Without a leader in the caravan of obsolescence,
we are halfway to the edge of our somewhere World—
everywhere is nowhere to a blind guide.

This is the warming residue of sturdy Nebraska,
the unperturbable epicenter
of old geology's perdurable vessel.

Bright sun, rich in yellow tapestry,
shining out its inner gold to illumine in regal ochre
the Mars-bound cold gray moon—deigns

to share its gratuitous warmth with us here below,
to shine its patient light upon winter's
weather-cracks unrepaired in ragged highways.

*

We of the new Third World, junked humanity,
can ill afford our ruptured surfaces. In a wreck
of government, one repair exposes every weakness:

Pot-holes are unfilled. Bridge approaches are compressed
ridges pushed against mis-aligned rotting spans.
The collapsed surface disguises the full wreck beneath.

>>>

A car skews a tire into the hidden jagged gap between
highway and paved shoulder. The wreck leaves twisted
bodies to flop bleeding into some unplowed field.

*

The First Two Worlds, the Passenger Classes:
The EEFO** and their red-capped maga-proles,
gather to pray together that their silver ark
never recover Earthly port:

For the Moon has eloped to the orbit of Mars,#
Where giddy wedding members toast the gleaming
Silver wake of the wild careening Moon,
Bound at warpèd speed for their brave new sphere,

For *imperial Powers, offspring of heav'n, Ethereal*
Virtues; Orb of imperial sweetness,
Trumpet the oranges## of their ample Host
From the bright sands of a Nambian### coast.

*Civilian Confiscation Corps.

**Executive/Entrepreneurial/Financial Orders.

#D. Trump, "We're going to Mars, of which the Moon is part."

##D. Trump, "The Oranges" of the Mueller report.

###D. Trump, on geography

I am aware that this poem collapses with a feeble Miltonic bleat at the end.
It is a sacrifice the poet is willing to make on behalf of topical verisimilitude.
It may not be fair that art must reflect its culture. But that's not the artist's fault,
entirely.
The whimper is not new to our governing, nor to poets' futile prognostications.
Consider Congress.

The Weather in Green: Evolution and Chance

after Mallarmé and before

Blue-white waves splash on the shore of a lake
stripped now of its beauty of trees.

Chugging chuffing coughing
iron blade up—
puffs of fragrant exhaust
whoof
along with the ghosts of not yet and far gone.

The memory of trees—
of their agonizing caesarian re-birth
split into boards for houses and shops
and the burning wooden towns of their age.

I am the *intra*locutor of ghosts—
my Dopplegänger's Doppel—
to connect what is gone with what is going, what
has already become revenant in the future—

I am equipped to tell no one, not even you—ah,

as though anyone can demand of time
more than a fey wheeze of memory
to control our manic vibrations,
the dys-tonal counterpoint to the euphony of waves,
music and soul
too far from pointless succor,

>>>

only sky and stars and no metaphor,
learning the dimensions of sky,
learning the dimensions of water,
the choreography of splashing from one element

                                        to the other,
the sad human dimension of failure,
the soaring dimension of again

          and again
                    and again.
                                        To pretend

to such control of my pen
I would have earned such vision
into what I write to allow words to be
as gentle with the image I try
to imagine of myself,
without which care words are no more
than spaces among falling leaves.

But sometimes hard times, these times—
words like weather rise out of the ground
Poseidon green,
tumble toward us with pulses
of their own—manic volition,
leprous inner glow—

words like bruised air moving wounded,
cornered gasping in a return to
Carboniferous miasma

>>>

a new dimension for old evolution
another playful hazard:

un coup de dés . . .

jamais . . . . non! . . .
n'abolira toujours!
le hazard.

(*a throw of the dice*
never . . . no! . . .
always! *abolishes*
chance.
[except when it doesn't])

Memento Mori: Among the Fossils

We sense the mortality of things: cattails,
the soft mullein on the lakeshore—the lakeshore,
as soft to eyes as to touch—the eyes themselves,
the mortality we share with what we see:

Next to the Cambrian trilobite, *Elrathia kingii*,
on my desk, the fossilized segment of an ancient
horsetail, *Calamites*, two inches in diameter,
from a plant that would have towered
above the delicate revenant horsetails
that grow on the lakeshore and by the road
to the mailbox between Carol and me
and the ferns whose ancestors grew along,

among, the ancestors of the horsetails,
Rhacophyton, along some yeasty lakeshore
to precede Carboniferous coalbeds, burned
to put the Iron Age on crushing wheels,
so that the sun would not set on the boot-tracks—
the railroads, the implanted colonial capitols,
the mine-fields and mausolea—the inexcusable
amnesia that propels the *Anthropocene* invasion.

"The end is quick," according to Eumaeus,
"sepulchered into the slow evolution of memorial
agate. We grow beautiful and virtuous again
all together in the same lithic kiln." *Memento.*

Eumaeus Questions the Fossils

Water working us gently warmly
away into the womb of Earth once more,
alone in the sea under the heave and tremor
of the geography of waves and swells,
alone with the shale-black orthocone,
alone with mosasaur, alone in the panic of her prey.

Or pike, above the disparate translucencies
of a lake a mile above the pillow of set lava balanced,
precarious above the igneous flow—
a knapped Folsom point, obscurant obsidian lens
through which to consider:

A scorpion after all
is company no more or less tender or "nice," you say,
than any company save what your young soul endows
than it had enjoyed by way of its primordial nature

never noticed
before your blossoming moment of grace—or—

hadrosaur's jaws oscillating back and forth,
so finely evolved
out of the dim birdiness of her ancestors—
back and forth in contemplative slowness
while the shadows of the shadows of poems,

>>>

undulate in the skull that sweeps slowly—
up and down,
back and forth from sedge to sky.

*

Dead to our childhood, the last sense of soul available,
we can no longer begin or pretend to hear the trees—
we can no longer reach the first branch to begin again.

Do you remember the clarity
high enough and in such danger of height and invention
when we embraced the tree for our only protection,
the good ache in the infinity
of our upward scramble maybe
way up a Cretaceous plane tree
in the farthest clearest distance—

see hear feel the hungry warmth of the consuming sun,
the chill of the twilit lorn horizon,
and then then then the sun.

The tree whispered back its name.
Unremembering, we listened.

*

We slaughter the flying creatures though we envy them,
descendants of the fourth freedom of evolution.

The lesser endowed among the evolved,
below the sky, only subsisting again, scavengers—

>>>

we will not fly!

And the fifth freedom?
the inspired human agon between a nomadic psyche
and the impenetrable orthodox—the genius!

But not now, not this year or era.
Far below the cave, the dug tomb—
the undertomb of anxiety,
the rising fire, the silence of echo
the sound of caves that we may stand above . . .
and recall that extinction is no disgrace.

The end is quick, sepulchered
into the slow evolution of memorial agate.

We may grow beautiful and virtuous again
refined together in the same lithic kiln,

but maybe

*

better that

we walk out of the forest again—
avoid the wet lips of the drooping
edge of trees.

Out to the west is the open plain.
The sun shines from behind our

>>>

warming backs.

We can see ahead,
feel the warm comfort
stroke our backs.

In the forest we are secluded, safe
in the shadows of trees.

Out here we are vulnerable to the sun,
to what the sun may shine upon
that comes our way.

We will see whatever comes come.
We can prepare for it,
prepare our fear.

But in the trees we cannot see
what may come.

What is our fate that hasn't come is
our comfort—
that hasn't come.

Our safety comes from remembering
that that might be—
only our comfort is in our forgetting.

On the plain there is no forgetting.
Our eyes on the field of distant horizon

>>>

remember for us.

Better that
we return to the forest.

Better that
we turn and go out onto the plain.

Better that we return,
that we turn.
Better . . .
better . . .

or . . . yes . . . ?

only better

but better enough

to keep care aware

Scythe of Peace

Combat helicopters range overhead.
The omnivorous grace of military aggression.
Earnest-eyed Powers and Thrones drone,
hunting hard for something
to protect their feeble nation from.

In a public garden I sit, being un-
threatened by this casual protection.
A mother and two small boys play nearby.
Spring flowers are starting to bloom.

"Don't move!"

1. *January 2016*
Our hired sailboat glides in white submissiveness
by the rock-strewn wreckage
that disguises the Navy's submarine dry-dock.

We bow our heads, not in homage
but to soothe the inner and guilty temptations
of our touristical curiosity.

We salute without motion the megalodon subterfuge
whose apparent job for the nation's security
is the confiscation of tourist cameras.

We confiscate our own cameras.

>>>

Locking up our cameras with our consciences,
we display the instincts of food.

2. *August 1961*

Before we embarked for a harbor tour
several wars and a half century ago
my inquisitive touring father
asked a Navy officer, "What's
all that stuff under the tarp
on the ship over there?"

The young officer smiled lieutenantly.
He responded in an official tone,
a well-armed docent,
not unfriendly, not unthreatening
"That is stuff under a tarp"—
"Sir"

The officer smiled then, satisfied.
My father deigned not to peek beneath the official humor.

"Don't move!"

3. *June 2020*

What exists of our nation now—
that which is not stuff under a tarp,
a very big and very thick and incendiary canvas?

One finger on the Tweeter button,
one finger on the red button,

>>>

our vaguely elected prepares to play the world
like a playroom full of slot-cars,
bathtub battleships, model airplanes, toy tanks, lead soldiers—
a small child's elfin trigger finger

aimed at tiny plastic populations poised for melting.
Polaris missiles threaten
to erupt from among innocent bubbles in his tub.

"Don't move!"

*

O, Mighty, hear our Public Prayer:
Allow us to protect ourselves instead, O Lord of Hosts,
from all the Hosts that contend to protect us.
Go all *ye quietly out together and let us close*
the door adamantly behind thee. And lock it!
Amen?
Amen.

Subjectory

This sinking gray bubble of clogged feathers
on the surface of Shallow Lake,
water-logged feathers of blue heron
only a quarter of the corpse
above the surface now,
three quarters down aimed toward the adventure
of sinking forever.

Its spindle legs fulcrum its appetites no more
nor is its triggered beak any danger
to frogs or minnows or baby ducks and loons—
or perch or bluegill or rock bass
once indifferent to living,
now guaranteed their red gills for some life more.

The cartridge of head, matted plume, bullet of beak
aim the rest of the bird down
where its gray disguise will disappear
entire into the masking muck beneath
the lily pads and cabbage weed.

Bubbles of methane
signaling the blue heron's slow entry into
the afterworld of gray peat—
oil, coal, immortality
or new fire—new gray ash,
a nativity of loam.

Icarus Rising

Part V

On Earth

George Santayana: *I am an ignorant man,*
almost a poet.

Eumaeus: *To be a poet is to become*
less than ignorant.

The poet works his words
from beneath his ignorance

without leaving the appendix
of his ignorance behind.

In the library
we exchange our greeting and our places and
you reach for your well-equipped walker.

You stop to ask me,
the only poet handy at the moment,
about the six-line poem
you had found in your late husband's financial papers.

You would like to know who wrote it,
if not he.
I'd like to help.
I'd like to see the poem.

But I think I do see it, or some part of it
in my irresponsible fashion.
Whatever it is, whoever wrote it, and
whatever it says, it is your poem.

It was written for your approval,
your memory, your close attachment.
What is so close to you as this has become
cannot have been written for anyone else.

Not anymore, until perhaps
you finish sharing it
with someone else, and it belongs,
rather like love,
to each of you.

Words with Heraclitus, 3

They say that the sun has been
865,000 miles wide

almost all the long eons since its birth.
To Heraclitus the sun is one foot wide.

In another two and a half millennia
will the sun be that much narrower

by geometric measure and moral erosion
or humans that much greater?

Will humans then be able to see
the sun as it is, or ourselves as we are?

Two of Us Talk Mortality

across 2 1/2 centuries

1. Seventh July 1764 (Francis, 74 years of age)

Swam this afternoon.
Nathaniel is still dead.
Six years?

Swam is not exact, I don't suppose.
The fear of leg cramps.
Even in the shallows.

Above my waist
the water is deep enough that I might
not have body-weight to push the cramp out.

—Are you getting this, Richard?—

*

2. July 22, 2018 (Richard, 74 years of age)

I keep my great-grandmother's caul
in a leather wallet
and I know therefore that I cannot drown.

I did not know my great-grandmother.
But my grandmother's reminiscences
indicate to me that her mother

was not to be trusted with any future

>>>

that she, my great-grandmother,
had not invented—

who invented only for herself
before she disappeared
into the oblivion of the Fens.

*

3. 21 August 1789 (Francis, 89 years of age)

The sky is clear.
Drifting pillows of new-born cloud.
Blue. My mind

and the sky are clear.
One more than the other.
One cannot say . . . one

cannot say.
The other *will* not say.
Which is which

is which
. . .
?

Where You Can't See It

"When you're in the desert,"
my grandfather says again,
"never put any part of your body
where you can't see it."

And while I try
to sort out the parts of my body
that are most likely to wander out of sight
and while I try
to sort out the parts of my body
that I can't see anyway,
and while I try

to consider what sorts of cracks, crevices, ledges,
or maybe beckoning abandoned mine shafts
that I might match
with parts of my body that I can't see,
some of which I have learned
to be embarrassed by anyway,

I slide on my rump down
the side of a cactus-lined arroyo toward
whatever hiding biting or stinging creature
might be waiting at the bottom
under some shading rock to free me from some part,
from embarrassment,
from my personal part in the shining spectacle

>>>

of speedy evolution that is before me
in all this new Russian roulette of desert.

I am something small again
or maybe without body parts at all
to worry myself about
or my grandfather about,
except maybe eyes,

except maybe ears for when the quail murmur
and other ears maybe
to listen to the absolute nothing
between the quail's murmur and the dove's keen.

The little cave in the wall of the arroyo
was dug out from under an old mesquite
in some succession of flash floods.
The cave mouth always faces east.

Behind me
as I face the east as well
the mesquite's tap root drills down
through sand and around rock after rock
and maybe even around some unbroken strata
left over from the last miracle of shallow sea.

Seventy feet, ninety,
the root augers down.

"My life is a key that has finally found its lock"

The older man deals in cars.
Vermont wry, soft-and-gentle spoken,
he sports the cornerless integrity
of the Yankee peddler.
He disguises his honesty
to protect the distraction
his fair offer might incur.

Today he pretends to rest a deal's success
on the drear fate of a toss-off bet:
"You wanna go double or nothing?"
when either double or nothing
could be part of a ritual comedy
to liven a contract already arranged.

At his side the guileless witness,
the bewildered new son-in-law—
newly attuned to the fascination of dire chance
and daily enthralled with the easy dash
of his newly mantled Ur-Father—
will fail to notice the unwritten
agreement between dealer and dealt-to,
old friends pretending antagonism,

not see that the actual bet,
nodded over and winked to,
entails no more than the post-deal drink,

>>>

when sacrificing a cheap “double-or”
promises another season's worth
of Yankee sacrament and the splendor
of the next year's gleaming model:

“Powerglide”
fuels a man's longing for speed in grace,
feeds the son-in-law's for,
if not mythos,
at least something manly and free
in his domestic novelty,
his shaky future—
his hope that he will play at least a bit part
of all that he may never learn to meet.

Board Walking, a Bit Part

My uncle Jim walks slowly by his garage
lugging two boards once
painted white, now
partly still white,
partly the mildew gray/
green of hapward decay—

like the nature of his walk,
partly still limber, partly
the calm revelation of his age
stumbling once, reminding him
of the calm revelation of dotage,
our final passive adventure.

Jim is eighty-nine in human years.
I don't know how old the boards
are in board years,
but I think they are not long
for our humid world,
no more than their diminishing strength
left somewhere behind the garage—

the calm revelation to all of us,
of the age of youth and dying,
evolution by extrapolating
from slow-walking observation.

Bison Head in Datil

Mid-August, 1962

An annual stop in Datil,
another burger, greasy fries—
greasy food-and-fuel-stop
defacing in human desperation
the raw beauty of an abandoned
stretch of desert.

Another summer visit
with the buffalo head mounted
on the smoke-blackened wall by the door,
sweat-shiny
with years of griddle-smoke
since its petty execution

by some city-hunter with a rifle
and just enough space
between technology and the beast
to get a shot off
into the Pleistocene heart
a few sunny yards away—

a cringing broadside.

Dad's '58 Fleetwood,
as misnamed as the buffalo is,
the car a bison-*manque*,

>>>

lumbering on Firestones
that flobber and slip on
soggy shocks and tarmac.

Jack gets to hold tight
to the over-reamed battery cables,
tight to the terminals—
Don't touch the metal!—
dead dangerous game so close
to dead dangerous game,

the miracle of the bison's agility
and its impossible strength
and will—
the lumbering
morbid-obese Cadillac
desiccating with us
in the petrified grime of industry.

Never Enough Air

Fentons Folly, summer 1949

"You know I can't—
can't breathe
when you keep all the windows shut!"

My mother's consumption is
always severe
but only mind-deep.

All the windows here are wide open
on three sides of the screen-porch,
the porch open as it was always

open before my father fiddled in
his chaos of odd-angled windows.
Only one glass pane then in our new door.

The single glass pane reminds me now
of the false place outside—the world's hot war

only a storm-past zephyr,
Korean conflict a sticky miasma—bloody
cypher of decades of cold to come.

We in the part of America
we claim as America
are faithlessly victorious.

>>>

We hide in plain sight behind glass,
sheltered in our porch,
east-facing

in a crisp wind from the west
that we'd have to think to face
before we discover the source of cooling air.

Un bel di vedremo

Mostly, when my mother sang
she sang alone in her alien kitchen.
Songs from *The Student Prince* she had sung
for a performance in high school.
All of the songs,
all sung to her unrequiteful emptiness.

Her barren stage a kitchen sink,
store-bought green tomatoes
softening three by three
in boxes trapped in cellophane
on the winter-shaded windowsill.

*

No one else at Washburn High could sing a lick.
My mother's voice,
so young then in late adolescence,
was enchanting.
Incantevole.

But my mother couldn't act a lick.
Cognition paralyzed,
she wandered around the stage
a pottering extra.
She took over every song,
her voice flew like a soul:

incantevole.

>>>

My mother was enchanting.
She sang alone
what she had picked up from Puccini:

Mimi's arias.
Madame Butterfly.
Sixty-five years after she sacrificed
our voices to utility
I cannot listen to "Un bel di."

Ah, I must listen to "Un bel di"
somehow to share the beauty
and hazard an attempt to court some vain
corrective memory of their shared and single horror.

*

My mother was enchanting.
She sang from the scullery
of women's forlorn sublime.
They sang,
a duet of a single voice in two souls.

They each know that their aria is about death:
theirs shared.
Butterfly sings of her lover's return,
Pinkerton gone forever
to her deadly/sublime belief.

One fine day and soon,
she would take their lives.

>>>

The two women together sing
their lonely way out of deadly routine,
sing into that fine day,
sing their common way out of life.

Together or apart, sharing
the life-long suicide that is beauty,
together as one they remain enchanting.
And I am living to become their last survivor—

*

Mi metto là sul ciglio del colle e aspetto,
on the edge,
like Odysseus staring out at the fruitless sea,
e aspetto gran tempo.

Den Milda Flickan Who Saved Me from the Martians

For Lacy and Emmy and their friends the grace
they live to share

i betänklig spel for such as we were,
my father and I exercising
memories, for en svensk far och son
so close to intimacy
that we risked again the numb
distance of our delod ångest. But

my father and I sat reminiscing
about our old home,
the artifact and memories we cared
to keep in common
in desperate lieu of the many facts we
preferred to leave to the vicarious
facts of fiction.

i berättelse,
I thought about Steve's big sister
for the first time in many years,
whose name we two couldn't recall,
and how we little kids liked her and how she
was the person to escort us,
walking all the way
through town at night
to see *The War of the Worlds.*

After the movie Steve's big sister,

>>>

too kind to show kindness,
let us walk heroically ahead of her
through the elastic red shadows of the night,
our fear screwed beyond the few red stop lights
toward that Martian eye.

Dad said then,
who was not of a generation to know the polite terms,
"You know she wasn't quite right?
She was, well, different, I guess you'd say?"
I did not,

and I don't, and I still
can't see the features of her soft face,
hooded eyes behind the glasses
that were more of her
than I had ever known,
and now I wonder if I ever saw,

and I wonder,
searching for her face, and
facing the red Martian again for a second,

have I been that obtuse,
or getting a little senile now, or
merely escaping discourtesy,
that I still can't see her face
behind her glasses—
or her grace?

But, because I know how much

>>>

easing my fear would matter to Steve's big sister,
how little not remembering her name,
the Martian in me withers and dies,
but only away.

Even in fiction,
especially in fiction,
especially in the fictions
we cannot help but re-invent,
while we re-invent our protective accounts,

some conversations,
red-eyed in the night, stay with us,
walk just ahead toward the red
horizon of en ouppnäelig
grynning.

En Musiklärare

for Loren Milton Sederstrom

A sample tea tin—"Celestial Seasonings"—
himmelska kryddor—a buried souvenir now,

a token-worth of my father's ashes inside,
lies tucked behind one window framing-board
he installed in the lumberjack's moonshine
shack he turned into a family cabin by hand
and humor, påstridig, städlig ensam.

It fits the serendipity of the one place
his fragile humor was never forced,
though his few best jokes, or his wittier
facility for modest gesture, had dissolved
in a mute sigh forty years before he died.

We doubt—those of us who Scotch-taped
these ashes into a bad and fitting pun forever,
that the man would argue its fitness much
in spite of the lost years sacrificed
to self-inflicted bourgeois scrupulosity,

upward and away from the hapless rejection
of the teaching he loved and the music
he ceased to play or hear, all sacrificed
for the income and rigors of business,
the veneering of his guileless conscience,

>>>

and the last years of stroke-inflicted peace—
that the found humor we try too late to share
may still reflect the founder of this room:
the mock emblem, the scant apologetics
of my läppisch attempt at memorial.

I Still Dream, After All

Blanket hanging out on a window ledge,
sheets scattered like faded cumuli—
if clouds could withstand a Bendix washer—
Aunt Nancy's bedstead and mattress
is exposed to its history and its geology
and a promise of painful demolition,
should the current victim awaken.

The lathed abraded spindles of head and foot
rack the tortured frame of Nancy's mattress.
Black and white ticking in narrow stripes
count themselves down from end to end,
like sullen angels with dirty faces.

Black and white stripes seem to bend
around the lumps in the mattress like
plow furrows in a Minnesota farm on a day
that beckons a leprous green thunderhead.

Untenanted, the mattress fails to betray
the pinball field of freed spring tips,
but I know so well where they are
that when I lie down tonight I will not
need to think ahead where I will curl my body
to avoid the bare point that, avoided,
will give me to dream in a pattern
of falling that gives the idle dream purpose,

>>>

the flight for freedom among piloting clouds.

And I do dream, and I do set myself free
from the bonds of what the mattress
has no choice but to mean for me.
But I also dream that it will come time
for me to dream at last of what will come
of my wings when the next spring
sizzles into my discoloring horizon.

Toad and Thunderheads

with Carol

We watch the last exploding thunderheads
plow to the East, and clouds and breeze
ease us back to the lee of our high summer calm.

You rake at storm debris to ignite another
cooking fire, at one with nature again, nurturing
your small portion of our windblown Earth.

A small toad distracts your work, jumps into your pile
of rakings for its security, and you gently, gently
edge it into some undergrowth whose fate isn't fire.

You talk together—at least you talk. Toad responds
in its slow way. I am still watching thunderheads
in their slow way too—and talk just a bit.

I tend ephemera, passing and past, while you
tend to this stubborn bloom of vitality.

Aspen

summer 2008

Here's how well we work together,
not always, you understand,
but most of the time,
especially when we're not paying attention.

When we came across the aspen
the morning's unweatherly tornado had spread
broken and naked across the drive,
I didn't have to say a thing.

"We'll get the chain saw," Carol said.

I limbed out the broken trunk
while Carol dragged
the gangly pieces into the woods.

Then I cut up the body of the tree
and we both finished the job.

And it is only now
when she and I are—
well, only a couple of towns apart
and only for the rest of this week—

it is only now that I have used words like
body and *limbs* and *naked*

>>>

and maybe especially *gangly,*
when I have all but given
the downed aspen a name,
that I sense that I am
being trained somehow—
I don't know how—for grief.

I read yesterday,
was reminded,
that Elinor Frost died
when Robert was just my age.
Elinor and Robert had been married
just as long as Carol and I have.

Frost's lunatic grief
left him as helpless as the aspen spread
out in the woods hidden
beyond the side of the road.

We work together in such company as that,
Carol, I,
the aspen and our histories,
our acquaintances in labor and thought,
the constant work
to revive the fallen in ourselves.

The Fourth Deer

Carol whispered from among
the season's last raspberries,
and we stopped in honor
of three velvet-antlered stags,
themselves stopped in timid
honor at our attention.

They moved on, or seemed to.
Had almost dissolved
when Carol stopped us again.
Like a new dimension, a fourth stag!
But the others had gone beyond
the rise to the next privacy.

So we stood here, Carol and I,
in the midst of raspberry bushes,
birch, aspen, time, and quandary.
Was he one of the first three,
or truly another, now gone too?
Were there three or four?

Were there no deer at all
where three or four will always be?
Do those features obscure time
for a time of trance now,
or obliterate an end to time itself?
How can it matter, to us?

>>>

How can it matter to *our* deer,
who did not cavil over
a count of *their* humans?
I suppose we will never know
how many stags possessed us
in those few minutes.

It matters only that they *are*,
maybe waiting for us
to stay with them still,
who kindly taught us for a moment
how to forget our intrusive tally
for the gracious matter of silence,

to re-create out of the bounds
of memory our common elders'
shared decorum, to abandon time
to landscape shared, to share
the supple courtesy and make
moments of perfect language—

not a word.

But then the benediction
of such sound as the deer have shared
with us—a shuffle in the undergrowth—
white tails like numena disappearing
offer us a sign of evolved deceit:
acknowledge appropriate dignity.

>>>

Invite the visiting predator—
honor us with the chance to attack,
misdirect us to miss the mortal heart.
To arm us with a potential of intent
unintended is to invite us to share
the touch of common fate.

The Relativity of Morning

It is gravity of course and off course.
This pre-dawn morning, gravity
is adventuring only for us together.

Tonight the moon somewhere among
the stars caught as if together in some shadow
of nothing in particular a few feet above
the sister shadow of a mesa, stars drift
in the soft lightlessness of cholla spines,

gravity gently pulling whicheverway
at the blue-tinsel shadowglow bending
back at the almost light—some of it,
just enough of it to draw into the horizon—

enough that when the morning lumen
almost begins to show, and a reserve of
yesterlight pulls up a mountain range—

the range that disappears in the just cause
of focused lightspeed pulled toward a mirage
in more solid light, the drifting range
deposited on a disconnected distance—

rises to observe gravity and generate
what is warming again in our bodies
from evaporating drowse caught

>>>

in a fleecy coil of its refractive trail,

drawn carelessly somewhereward
with the last drops of our mutual
night of singular dream. Gravity,
kindly nudging our arms and our bodies,
binds us together to play out the dawn.

Afterward

Just in Case . . .

What May Interfere with Sleep

That non-arrangement of pine knots in the beam
I have been looking at from my bed since I was a small child
after my father had forced it up there to support us—
in great inconvenience and trouble and not a little
pain in one shoulder and that bad knee of his—
has always looked to me . . .

but this is a distraction and an inconvenience to an old man
and lover of peace, or at least decorum—
like a revolver ready to cock, eager to exact such damage
as I shall gladly and finally not miss
in the oblivion that is the absence of the miseries
of the century I was brought to

by birth, rearing, education, and love,
the oblivion that is the absence of
cruelty, war, torture of body, torture of mind—
minds of the imprisoned, the mortally threatened,
the starved for food, for knowledge—brought to
the many moments of the freedom I have squandered.

Oblivion is the absence of consciousness,
the absence of absence, the absence of oblivion.
No distraction
always more and less than whole can be complete.
Distraction can only be *liable* to completion,
never more, never less than grace.

>>>

The grace we hunger for in a long life
we find at last may be as painful as faith,
as comforting as doubt.
Still, it is grace, as beautiful as physics,
the distracting tension that keeps us alive:
the shaman's dramatic charm against completion.

I Would Not Care to Die Completed

Last night you were explaining
what you and your busted ankle
require to get you from here to your garden
and the inconvenience this episode has proved to be,
but not the pain.

You added that it was *only* an inconvenience,
not permanent, and that "You learn."
And that's when I thought of something I had written
in the back of some poet's book.
Was it James Wright? Yes—I looked. Good company here.

"I would not care to die completed" I wrote—
I'd like to see myself lying in my bed
propped up on several down-filled pillows.
My grandmother's—my great grandmother's—
eiderdown comforter is still soft and light.

The air is light, and a glitter of dust-motes moves
like a question in the small voice of air, like
angels no bigger than atoms of oxygen.
We share these last hours or moments—
but they,

quieter than oxygen released for the occasion
from the head of their infinite kingdom,
the head of that pin,

>>>

enough voice to breathe soundlessly
the message for and from stunned Elijah,

for the dying poet too in still small ecstasy
unencumbered by harp or trumpet or even tongue.
The comfortable old doubter is propped
on the down pillows high enough to remind him
not of angelic presences

but of the air that moves them,
and moves his breath, filters his breathing.
There should be flowers, but not inside,
perhaps the usual summer's decorous blue
migration of creeping bellflowers

that work their seasonal way around the house,
not to show themselves off nor to show off the house
but to remind me lying there
of their habit of inhabiting abandoned houses and foundations
and the proper blue gardens of some other century,

gone to seed and mongrel life
that will not stop to be monumental,
never stop nor allow for completion
while I wait for that unnatural punctuation
:

out of my control and therefore out of my range
of interests at the ultimate nonce.
I might startle myself away from

>>>

the communing motes and the air that lights them
and think to myself alone, or maybe ask

"What is it?" and answer or try or pretend.
Yes, pretend—the poet's daily bread. One breath
is never like another. The task is tasting each
and tasting the silence in the mortal distance
between, and tasting the distance itself.

But If . . .

Soliloquy by the Candle-Light of Day

for Caedmon

I wake up again to clouds—
clouds, dull linens of clouds,
to lines, words of poems,
soft dull linens of words

on the fore and plowing edge of a determined
raft of dream surging down some sleep-powered wake.
I knew I could wake up—get up,
fumble for one of the pencils on my bedside table

and one of the folded shirt-pocket size
discarded memories of scarified paper,
write the words or the lines or
once or twice

lines of music whose delicacies I cannot notate
nor ever learned how.
But I knew alerted by the clear spray of ideas now
that I would remember in the morning.

>>>

I never did. Did you? Ever?
But one night I dreamt some of those words again
or lines or prisms of image in the foam of notes.
Then I dreamt that I got up

got out of bed
picked up a pencil
found a folded paper
and then I dreamt that I wrote it all down.

All and beautiful—and all in a murky second gone into the foam.
I've never dreamt such dream again
but some urge behind the surge of dream told me
to write for the fabric of dream, the linen shadows of clouds,

anything at all, anything away from my sullen old silence.
Though it is a grace of old age the dream has been good,
a faith in dreams of embers all these lights ago—the
"highest candle lights in the dark,"

which dark
needs no more than a candle
and less
to read into the wakening heaves of breath a new old life.

*

>>>

I would live so long as to share with Tomas Tranströmer:

jag är just den plats
där skapelsen arbetar på sig själv. . . .
Jag är vändkorset.(x)

:

Cathartes aura in Opere et Veritate

for David Chorlton
and for Challie Facemire

1

Squat junipers dot valley and mountainside
in the desert view from David's photo.

Juniper boughs, cool green on the dexter side of the landscape,
some tree, in shadow, arrests a partial symmetry on the sinister.

Symmetry is a human craving, desperate and consoling.
Below notice to the vulture

whose consolation is to perch atop the skeleton
of another juniper, the human camera's

2

middle focus.
A purification.

It is desert.
Desert translates light to clean air and arid breeze.

3

That sere, petrified gray branch will support the vulture
and generations of vultures to come.

The vulture's bland attention purports a view
that two beings understand the fortunate life of the vulture.

>>>

One is the photographer
who frames the subtle asymmetric wonder of the vulture's world.

The other is the vulture, who sees and tastes that world
and its symmetric Stygian counter-world: like as not the same
place.

4

Ah, but one other being too—an obfuscated interlocutor:
the poet: vulture's dys-symmetric confidante.

To Wish We Were Eumaeus, Well Descended

I. Eumaeus Tends

The old dog will come back or he will not.
It does not matter,
not to the dog, not to me.
Not to my pigs.

If they were sheep. Sheep are different.
With sheep the dog has two choices.
The dog will herd the sheep. Or
the dog will kill a sheep. Maybe two.

With pigs it is different.
No dog will herd pigs. Pigs won't stand for it.
No dog will kill a pig. Dogs know the danger.
Especially an old dog. Especially this old dog.

He will come back though, unless he has died.
I think he won't die.
If it were me . . . but I have young dogs.
I don't need this dog.

Pigs almost never stray from the trough.
A pig far from the trough will either starve
or he will learn to kill the biggest dog.
The dog doesn't need me. In me

the dog has no one to die for, no one to live for. So.

>>>

The dog will return. And if
after these years the master himself should return
then the dog can make his choice.

He will choose to see the master, or
he will choose to die. Or some god will choose.
With me, the dog has no reason to choose.
He will come back.

And I?
I will save the fattest pig for the master.
Then I will make my choice.
Or I will not.

*

II. Descendant

If I were Eumaeus
I would not expect you to be Odysseus.
I would greet you when I saw you, whoever you be.

Still, though not Eumaeus,
I would hope to have fed you anyway
in and out of any name.

But I am only . . . what?
an old man with a room full of books,
papers

and I am too tired of my welter
of invisible poverties. Before I die I would

>>>

promise to leave you some cleared room,

wherever you are and however
you manage to get to the room
and how you choose to fill it.

You will remember perhaps,
and I may remind you,
that I have tried to leave you, Eumaeus,

that good man of hospitality—
gentle man, gentle mind,
more than spirit though:

To stand and wait remains a worthy calling,
and a simple dinner will serve,
especially those

who leave nor print nor scar on Earth
. . .

For Doigt Plie, for Eumaeus, for Caedmon, for Francesco, for Letitia, for Hugh and Vera and Francis Fenton, for Bartleby, for Joseph Grand, for Herman who failed to quit, for Emily still learning. For all of us who honor the pages of the ***Codex****.*

Endnotes

(i) Heraclitus, Fragments, Trans. Brooks Haxton

(ii) When one has come as far as I in futility
each word is more fascinating.

(iii) The tiny word you
perhaps a pearl of glass . . .
The large word I
perhaps a flint shard . . .

Gunnar Ekelöf, from *Songs of Something Else*,
trans., James Larson and Leonard Nathan.

(iv)

Churches,
dome-growths,
their facades
petrified gardens of symbols . . .

Octavio Paz, "Nocturno de San Ildefonso"

(v) Everything that has light casts a shadow,
Light and shadow go hand in hand.

But if the flame itself has no shadow,
Does the candle's flame really have light?

Alberto Blanco, "Teoria de conjuntos,"
trans., Gustavo V. Segade, in *Reversible Monuments.*

(vi) p. 63. You seek the eternal in the rational?
p. 64. I seek in the temporal the irrational.

Gunnar Ekelöf, *En Mölna-Elegi.*

(vii) They buried her in the family tomb
and in the depths the dust
of what was once her husband
trembled:
joy for the living
is sorrow for the dead.

Octavio Paz, "Epitaphio de una vieja"
Quotations trans., Eliot Weinberger,
The Collected Poems of Octavio Paz, 1957-1987

(viii) "Skäms inte för att du är människa, var stolt!
Inne i dig öppnar sig valv bakom valv oädligt.
Du blir aldrig färdig, och det är som det skall."

Tomas Tranströmer, "Romanska Bägar,"
("Romanesque Arches"), Trans., Patty Crane

(ix) "Monkey Mountain," from Thomas Merton's version,
The Way of Chuang Tzu.

(x) I am the place
where creation is working itself out. . . .
I am the turnstile.

from *The Great Enigma*, trans. Robin Fulton.

www.ingramcontent.com/pod-product-compliance
Lightning Source LLC
LaVergne TN
LVHW090939080826
845145LV00003B/821

* 9 7 8 1 9 2 8 6 9 0 4 6 7 *